The *Inspirited Life*

A Conversation between Jesus and Nicodemus

Bernice Austin-Brutus

ISBN 978-1-63814-219-5 (Paperback)
ISBN 978-1-63814-220-1 (Digital)

Covenant Books, Inc.
11661 Hwy 707
Murrells Inlet, SC 29576
www.covenantbooks.com

TO GOD BE THE GLORY

For a few years now, I felt the power of the HOLY SPIRIT compelling me to expand upon the conversation between Jesus and Nicodemus. Every time I read the Gospel of John Chapter 3, or heard it read, the persuasion became stronger. I know there is power in this conversation and Jesus' invitation to be born again is an invitation to join GOD'S Kingdom and to begin to enjoy His lavish love poured over us through Jesus CHRIST. I dedicate this book to GOD, the Father, GOD, the Son and GOD, The Holy Spirit.

I will be forever grateful to my daughter, Dr. Jonelle Bertrand for her confidence and dogmatic approach in believing that I could author this book and capture the life-changing words of Jesus when I doubted. To my grandchildren, Savion for his scholastic advice and Jelise for employing her artistic skills in designing the cover of this book. May GOD continue to empower you both with wisdom. To my late parents, Enid and Hubert Austin, grandparents, Elizabeth Austin, Samuel and Eliza Alleyne who were instrumental in teaching me the love of GOD by words and deeds.

To all my family and friends, particularly Melanie Taylor–Williams who willingly engaged her professional critique of the early manuscript. To Maureen Sharples and Gurmay E. Fraser, author of *Love me or Leave Me and My Journey to Spiritual Restoration*. for believing in me and bolstering my faith. To the Sheriff family who were excited at the proposition and wished me success. My heartfelt thanks.

Contents

Introduction

The conversation between Jesus and Nicodemus in John's gospel reveals the final, divine, dynamic drama of God's complete deliverance of the human race from the fall—humanity's salvation. Under the curse of sin, humans live in a substandard state, far below God's original plan, purpose, and potential for His prime creation. Humanity, originally created in honor, exercised the greatest gift of free will and chose to live apart from the source of its origin— God. Once this source was disconnected, humans became dishonored, disgraced and died. All heaven mourned, and a demonstration of this grief is recorded in the Gospel of John at Lazarus's death. "And Jesus wept" (John 11:35 CSB).

However, since humans die as a consequence of all of nature, the Creator, according to His indescribable love, determined not to abandon His creation but to recreate the human race. Therefore, through His only begotten Son, Jesus—who became incarnate, overcame death, rose, and returned to heaven with His nail-scarred body—alas, the human template resides in the heavens, redeemed and restored, having victoriously passed through the portals of death. Consequently, when Jesus ascended, the Holy Spirit descended to now quicken and change the mortal humanity (rebirth) into immortality (Romans 8:11). A new life that is capable of exercising the gift of free will, now principled by the power of the Holy Spirit in making the best choice—God (Philippians 2:9–11).

Mathew introduces his gospel with the human genealogy of Jesus by periods of fourteen generations, beginning from Abraham to his appointed guardian, Joseph, who became the Virgin Mary's husband. In Jesus' human nature, His biological line is not exempt from questionable characters as Jacob, Rahab, and Tamar who many, if given the opportunity, would rather not select to be in their ancestral line. The inclusion of these characters demonstrates the fact that Jesus, who is holy as in His divine nature, became contaminated with our sins through His human nature and thus became akin to us. God has added our names to His human genealogy, and we must add our names to God's spiritual genealogy as born-again believers.

On the other hand, we who are baptized have received the Holy Spirit. At Jesus' baptism in the River Jordan, God declared that Jesus is His beloved Son in whom He is well pleased. Born-again believers must insert their names in this declaration of love by God who has bestowed His divine nature on us as well. Under this divine status, believers may legitimately pray, "Our Father who art in heaven, hallowed be thy name." Hence, believers, like Jesus, consist of two natures, that of divine and human.

Jesus died in order to bring humanity back to dwell with God the Father, God the Son, and God the Holy Spirit. Because Jesus took on our humanity, rose from the dead with his nail-scarred body, and ascended to heaven, our humanity is now elevated and has taken its place in the heavenly places. Hence, since humanity went up, the Spirit came down, giving humanity new status (rebirth).

The Holy Spirit given to Christians is post-resurrection. Those baptized are born again by the power of the Spirit who raised Jesus from the dead. Then this conquering Spirit grants believers a new birth—the "inspiritation" (in'spirit ta SHen). Hence, one is no longer only human but exists with a dual nature, as was Jesus at His birth. This spiritual nature elevates Christians to become children of God and thus joint heirs with Jesus in the kingdom of God (Timothy 1:6–8). the life of the Spirit is altogether rich because it produces fruit here on earth.

The three ages reflect the Holy Trinity. God is manifested in the Old Testament with its prophets, priests, and kings. Jesus manifesting in human form ushers in the second age, consisting of the four synoptic gospels, letters, revelation, and the power of the Son's salvation. The Holy Spirit revealed in the third age resides in all born-again believers and the organization of the church which began on the day of Pentecost (Acts 2).

"Inspiritation"

One of the tenets of the Christian faith is that Jesus is the Son of God and Savior of the world. Jesus left His heavenly abode to come down to earth and took on human nature in order to save humanity. Jesus was born of the Virgin Mary as predicted by the Angel Gabriel. Therefore, Jesus is both human and divine; His divine nature originated from God in heaven and His human nature from the Virgin Mary who was, in all aspects, willing to be the mother of the Messiah. In a conversation with the Angel Gabriel, Mary was told that the power of the Holy Spirit would come upon her and she would bear a *son* (Luke 1:35). The angel also revealed to Mary that her yet-unborn son would inherit the dynasty of David, the great and well-known king of Israel of whom God referred to as "a man after my own heart" (1 Samuel 13:14).

Nicodemus was in the Jewish hierarchical tradition of leadership and a member of the Sanhedrin. He most likely heard about Jesus' acts of healing and authoritative teachings. This Jewish leader was distraught and had questions for Jesus. Nevertheless, he did not want to compromise his status in the community by seeming to consort with Jesus of Nazareth. As a result, he visited Jesus under the cover of darkness—by night. This book places in perspective the dynamic conversation between Jesus and Nicodemus of the power and privilege to be born-again. Through love, God created the world, and through love, He is determined to put humanity back in its proper prospective and purpose for which He created it. To be born-again is God admitting us to the highest level of existence on earth, which is to become like Jesus, with also a dual nature—human and divine. The divine nature is made possible by the inspiritation of the Holy Spirit. This is the abundant life that Jesus declared in the Scripture that He came to give humanity (John 10:10). The abundant life is made possible by the Holy Spirit of God whose kingdom has no boundaries. For the Spirit life is not under the auspices of time and cannot be controlled by time and its limits. Hence, the elevation to this level becomes a reality made possible by a new existence—being born-again.

Christianity has missed the most important and revolutionary declaration made by Jesus to Nicodemus that was captured in the Gospel of John, that he must be "born again." This invitation is explosive because Jesus is conferring on Nicodemus the ability to become a child of God. It is the opportunity of a lifetime for Nicodemus and all who believe in Jesus to advance from the fallen nature of Adam and to also take on the nature of a holy God. This is a declaration which some may argue is blasphemous, but the invitation comes from Jesus who came to earth for this very purpose.

God is determined that humans made in His image should not perish and that the devil must not have the last word (John 3:16). The invitation to this new state of existence is theologically supported by the Bible in many writings and letters of the Old and New Testament. John, known as the "beloved disciple," is the only gospel writer who recorded this status-changing, earth-shattering conversation of Jesus and Nicodemus. A conversation that indeed defines the true meaning of the word "gospel"— good news. The third chapter of John encompasses the entire New Testament and represents the complete resolve of God concerning the state of humanity and His intention to save the human race by giving us a second chance.

Those who believe in God are given the opportunity to be like Jesus, the Son of God, consisting of two natures—the human and the divine. As Jesus is incarnate, He is inviting Nicodemus to dwell under a new and wonderful existence. His disciples are now "inspirited"[1] by being born of the Holy Spirit. They have dual natures and must make every effort to develop the responsibilities of such wonderful possibilities of power and wisdom. Peter the apostle captures the gist of this conversation when he wrote, "Blessed be the God and Father of our Lord Jesus Christ, which according to his abundant mercy hath begotten us again unto a lively hope by the resurrection of Jesus Christ from the dead" (1 Peter 1:3). Peter states "begotten us again." Believers are given the opportunity to be born again.

The incarnation of Christ initiates the "inspiritation" of human beings. In Jesus' conversation with Nicodemus, it is revealed that humans must be reborn in order to inherit the kingdom of God. This is an invitation to accept

---

[1] "Inspirited" is a word I designed to explain the indwelling of the Holy Spirit in the born-again believer.

the birthing of the Holy Spirit in one's life so that each person may encounter God and receive the Holy Spirit who was referred to by the Angel Gabriel who greeted the Virgin Mary in the Gospel of Luke. John the Baptist prophesied about the inspiritation of humankind when he pronounced, "I baptize you with water unto repentance… he shall baptize you with the Holy Ghost and with fire" (Matthew 3:11). Jesus declared to Nicodemus, "Marvel not that I say unto thee, Ye must be born again" (John 3:7), signifying that he was born once and that was in human nature, and the "again" in Jesus' statement suggests a new birth by the Spirit from above. "You must be born of water and the spirit."

Nicodemus was unable to fathom the enormity and revelation of this declaration for rebirth by Christ. He was strictly in his human elements and nature. He failed to comprehend spirituality as well as its power as being part of the new creation. Creation that must evolve and flourish as a result of accepting Jesus' invitation to share in a new dual nature (human and divine). This is what I refer to as the "inspiritation" (perhaps a new word) to explain the opposite of Christ's incarnation (see footnote 1). Paul declared, "Therefore if any man be in Christ, he is a new creature, old things are passed away; behold all things are become new" (2 Corinthians 5:17). This new creature—the born-again believer—must leave the old life behind and begin exploring the possibilities and power of the Spirit life.

Praying in a church setting provides encouragement and benefits to members of the church as a spiritual community, but individual moments of quietude and meditation establish essential spiritual development and insight. This solitude or one on one with God empowers the disciple to see God more clearly and hear his voice more keenly and conditions the heart to obey readily. Spiritual directives given to a disciple and a subsequent prompt response to His request and render rapid progression and furtherance of the kingdom of God.

A likely example is that of Ananias (a Christian of the early church) when he was instructed by God the Holy Spirit to go to Straight Street and anoint Saul of Tarsus, a persecutor of the church, in order to restore his sight and baptize him. Ananias appealed to God about the dangerous reputation of Saul, who was persecuting the Christians in the early church, but God assured him that He had chosen Saul to become an apostle (Acts 9). Ananias obeyed God's directive, and Saul, who was renamed Paul, became a disciple and authored many letters of the New Testament and established several churches among the Gentiles living in Roman colonies. Through the ages, the Letters of Paul in the New Testament remain relevant in the exposition of God's love, the interpretation of the Old Testament prophesies, and the significance of the salvific work of Christ that have converted many people to Christianity. His writings have influenced several great theologians, including Martin Luther, the reformer of 1517, and Augustine. This was accomplished because of Ananias's obedience to the instructions of the Holy Spirit.

Discipline

Nicodemus's response to Jesus' statement "of being born again" is proof of the limitations of the human mind. He replied, "How can a person once grown old be born again? Surely he cannot reenter his mother's womb and be born again, can he?" This teacher of Israel was unable to stretch his mind beyond the sphere of his physical realm. Likewise, the Jews' resistance from following Jesus also attest to their spiritual limitations when they pondered how Jesus could give them His flesh to eat and His blood to drink. These retreating disciples refused to abandon their obscurity and chose instead to be controlled by their natural boundaries (John 6:52).

A question may be asked as to why the necessity to be born-again, and Paul aptly answered in 1 Corinthians 15, informing us that human nature cannot inherit the kingdom of God because its makeup is perishable. Perishability denotes the presence of time, and the kingdom of God transcends time. Therefore, the two are separate; the very human nature caught under the umbrella of time is scientifically impossible to dwell in timelessness, which is eternity. Because human nature, being perishable, denotes time, an expiration date. "This I declare, brothers; flesh and blood cannot inherit the kingdom of God, nor does corruption inherit incorruption" (1 Corinthians 15:50). The kingdom of God is imperishable, denoting the fact that its existence does not involve chrono time; there is no need for the clock in the Spirit world.

Paul's reasoning explains this important conversation between Jesus and Nicodemus. The disciple needs the spiritual nature as well in order to qualify for entrance into the kingdom of God. While the body perishes, the Spirit lives on in dimensions that possesses no corruption, for the Spirit is incorruptible. The Spirit is God who exists without any limits or reserve. Hence, the necessity for human nature to eventually change for future kingdom residence is apparent. In addition, while here on earth, human nature needs the Holy Spirit to prepare it not only for life in the future kingdom but to begin contributing to the kingdom here on earth. For this reason, in the Lord's Prayer, we are taught to say, "Thy kingdom come, thy will be done in earth as it is in heaven" (Matthew 6:10). The expansion of God's kingdom is the responsibility of the faithful born-again believer, prompting others to leave their temporary dwelling, human nature, and approach the marvelous light made possible by the Holy Spirit.

The inspiritation of Christians transforms the new person who becomes a follower of Christ and who must be conscious of his/her dual nature in the new life as a Christian. It is a challenge living with this dual nature where the flesh is in a state of constant opposition to the Spirit. The struggle is real, and the Christian is faced with the fact that these natures must cooperate with each other, as was seen in Christ. Christians must be alert at all times to maintain the balance of these natures which, at first, may be experienced as enmity between them. There may be a state of anxiety at some point in time when faced with the battle between the carnal and the spiritual. Oswald Chambers captures this new relationship: "If the Spirit detects anything in you that is wrong, He doesn't ask you to make it right; He only asks that you accept the light of truth, and then He will make it right" (Chambers 2000).[2]

This new relationship places everyone who believes "as children of God, inheritors of the kingdom of God and co-inheritors with Jesus in the heavenly kingdom" (Church of England 1992).[3] This is the very reason Jesus taught His disciples to pray by calling God this intimate and endearing salutation, "Our Father" (Abba) (Matthew 6:9). As Christians become adept to the Spirit, a relationship develops and becomes stronger by the many experiences and practices of communications with the Holy Spirit, *Spiritus Sanctus*. Thus, the flesh has no reason to object or engage in battle but to obey.

The fact is that God became man in the incarnation. Hence for us who follow Christ, we become spiritually proficient as we are inhabited by the Holy Spirit who is a part of the Godhead, the Holy Trinity. Therefore, we who are new creatures exercise supernatural powers manifested in Jesus Christ. For Jesus declared, "Verily, verily, I say unto you, He that believeth on me, the works that I do shall he do also; and greater works than these shall he do; because

---

[2] Oswald Chambers, *My Utmost for His Highest: Selections for the Year*, daily devotion, March 23.
[3] Church of England, *The Book of Common Prayer*.

I go unto my Father" (John 14:12). Thus, Christians enter into a new relationship with the Godhead being children of God and part of the divine holy family. This family relationship is corroborated in Jesus' declaration on the occasion of His glorious resurrection: "I ascend unto my Father, and your Father; and to my God, and your God" (John 20:17). This gives the Christian direct access to God not only as God but on an intimate level of association. Where sin had severed this intimate relationship between God and humanity in the garden of Eden, so by Christ's power of the resurrection, all who believe in Him have access to spiritual power and the ability to exercise such.

The truth of attaining mystical power is certainly and exclusively a result of inspiritation. This mysticism is achieved exclusively through the Holy Spirit as a result of being born again and manifested through the particular, peculiar, spiritual gifts distributed to each member of the family of God. The Holy Spirit is manifested in many and various ways as directed by God for His glory and His glory alone—*sola gloria*. God is in control and disperses the Holy Spirit as He deems appropriate as revealed in the Old Testament. Moses, inundated with the responsibilities of leading the Israelites from Egypt, appealed to God for help. The Scripture records that God declared, "And I will come down and talk with thee there; and I will take of the spirit which is upon thee and will put it upon them; and they shall bear the burden of the people with thee, that thou bear it not thyself alone" (Numbers 11:17). The Holy Spirit present in each follower of Christ bears witness to God at all times. The reply that Jesus sent to John the Baptist when

John had questions about Jesus' status is the criteria for all born-again believers. "Go your way, and tell John what things ye have seen and heard; how that the blind see, the lame walk, the lepers are cleansed, the deaf hear, the dead are raised, to the poor the gospel is preached" (Luke 7:22).

Our carnal nature is now extremely enhanced, and the combination of these natures (carnal and Spirit) creates the relationship of the brotherhood of Jesus. Thus, He is the firstborn of a long line of siblings dating from the first apostles and disciples to us today and to those who are yet to be born-again. The first letter of John informs us that we are children of God, and if we are the children of God, we Christians are reborn by the Spirit who is greater than anything this world has to offer because this indwelling Spirit is God (1 John 4:4). Therefore, Christians bear the nature of their Father and witness like brother Jesus to the power of God and His truth by the power of the Holy Spirit.

However, the position of the brotherhood of Jesus must never promote disrespect in any form. In families of old and even presently, in some societies, much respect is granted to the firstborn. On my maternal side of the family, my oldest uncle was always addressed as Brother Randolph by all his younger siblings. Due respect for Jesus is required at all seasons, as the Scripture informs, "That at the name of Jesus, every knee should bow, of things in heaven, and things in earth, and things under the earth" (Philippians 2:10). King David referred to Jesus as Lord although it was decreed that the Messiah in the parameter of human terms would be his descendant (Luke 20:42–44).

This concept distinguishes the legitimate from the illegitimate and informs those who would seek to acquire inspiritation by human efforts or other sources. An appropriate incident, known as simony in Acts of the Apostles, corroborates the possibility of persons wanting to possess the Holy Spirit by human manipulations. One man named Simon, after seeing the miracles done by the apostles, wanted to purchase it. "And when Simon saw that through laying on of the apostles' hands the Holy Ghost was given, he offered them money" (Acts 8:18). The inspiritation of man comes from God and God alone. God is eager to have us be part of His heavenly family of Father, Son, and Holy Spirit. In relationship with the Holy Trinity, one is inspired to speak words of peace, prophesy, healing, solitude, and peace. As the Scripture declares, God is Spirit, and those who worship Him must worship Him in Spirit and in truth (John 4:24).

Those who receive the Holy Spirit receives life and light and develops a personal relationship with God, a relationship that is experienced here on earth and extends to eternity. This relationship strengthens the Spirit and allows it to take control and influences the carnal nature so that a born-again believer is disciplined and alert, ever vigilant for that moment of weakness. "So I say, live by the Spirit, and you will not gratify the desires of the sinful nature. For the sinful nature desirers what is contrary to the Spirit" (Galatians 5:16). Therefore, the inspiritation of the Christian or being born-again implies that the new state of being belongs to God, becoming God's children. Jesus is

God's Son. Thus, the presence of the Holy Spirit gives us power to become children of God.

It is imperative that we ask for the gift of the Holy Spirit because God is ready and able to bestow Him to Christians. This is the best and most supreme gift we as Christians should desire. For in our sinful, mortal, fallen nature, we strive to give good gifts to our children and desire to have them prosper according to our devices. How much more invaluable is the gift from God, the *Almighty who was, who is, and who is to come* and who grants us the brightest and the best—the Holy Spirit?

The Holy Spirit promotes the work of God in the world through Christians. This is plainly recorded in Acts of the Apostles when He directed Barnabas and Saul to preach the gospel far beyond the boundaries of their surrounding neighborhood. These two apostles, tasked with extending the good news to the Gentiles, began the first missionary journey in Cyprus (Acts 13:2). This journey was the first of three missionary trips taken by Paul and began the subsequent construction of many churches along the paths of Roman territories and colonies. The spiritual care and development of these churches are recorded in the Scripture as letters. These missives form a significant part of the New Testament where Paul wrote many of his letters to the churches, encouraging and developing their faith and love for Christ and for one another. This directive of the Holy Spirit confirms the command given by Jesus to take the gospel into all the remote areas of the world. "But you will receive power when the Holy Spirit comes upon you, and you will be my witnesses in Jerusalem, throughout Judea and Samaria and to the ends of the earth" (Acts 1:8). Christians like Barnabas and Paul, empowered by the Holy Spirit, are commissioned to embark on missionary journeys for the sake of Christ and the gospel. If each Christian living today will obey this commission as a commitment to speak and live the gospel, this world will be greatly transformed.

The pastor of the church I attend always instructs that the parents of the newly baptized promote the celebration of their child's baptism—their born-again date. Just as it is customary to celebrate the natural-born birthdate, it is expedient for the celebration of the spiritual. The celebration is appropriate because we are reborn and recreated to possess the divine nature which complements our human one. As recorded in Zechariah, it is not by our own strength or power that miracles are done but by the power of the Holy Spirit (Zechariah 4:6). Christians must feel confident to utilize the power of the Holy Spirit to perform the works that Jesus did while He was among us. Studying the Bible is essential to developing this relationship with God through the Holy Spirit who directs and teaches us the true application of God's holy words. The Holy Spirit empowers every Christian to accomplish the full potential and develop the gifts given to each person. Seize the time that is available to develop this relationship which would grow not for our self-aggrandizement but in service to God and our fellow humans.

Water is often referred to as the presence of the Holy Spirit. Jesus' conversation with the woman at the well indicated that the water she should have asked for is the water of life—the Holy Spirit who is forever welling up in the Christian to accomplish all that God has in store for them and those they encounter on a daily basis. Tapping into the source of the Holy Spirit would soon become natural and essential to a believer's witness. Even in the face of fierce opposition and upheaval, believers can remain calm and collected in spite of the raging storms that surround us. Anchored in this power, the Christian demonstrates the power of God and His willingness to have us all relate to Him and place our faith in His power. Yet God's deliverance may not meet one's expectations, but it is necessary to accept it whether we understand it or not because God is God and, as the Scripture declares, "and his ways past finding out" (Romans 11:33). We will often be puzzled at the way prayers are answered—most often, not according to our human expectations. Yet with development of the relationship with the Holy Spirit, we will be amazed, readily accepting, and grateful of God's decisions.

God disciplines and teaches His children—the born again—like a child who has to be disciplined from time to time. Earlier in life, in the study of the Word, I wondered why God hardened Pharaoh's heart and made him very stubborn that he refused to release the Israelites. This stubbornness served as a teaching period for the Egyptians, the Israelites, as well as for us today. The ruler of Egypt, under no stretch of the imagination, was a match for God.

However, it was the time of school where God wanted to teach the Israelites that He is the only God to be worshipped, the God of power and might, not the gods of stone and brass made by human hands. God demonstrated His might and power to instill that He was the Creator of the materials that composed the Egyptian gods. For four hundred years, the children of Israel immersed under slavery in the culture of Egypt and witnessed the worship of idols and the political, military, and administrative might of this country. God deemed that it was time for them to return to the land of Canaan and to worship and trust in the God of their ancestors—Abraham, Isaac, and Jacob. Thus, God continues to teach and train the born-again to trust Him completely and exclusively in all areas of life. While Jesus lived among us, He demonstrated this same power. Like a newborn baby who needs to be taught and disciplined, God employs similar circumstances and divine-ordained incidents to mold us into the likeness of His Son.

I can attest to this training personally when, in retrospect, God engineered uncomfortable circumstances to cause me to return to my country. Instead of pursuing an opportunity to further my education in America, I returned home to South America. Shortly after my return, I married my fiancé who was a hardworking public servant and was blessed with two children. My husband had helped his widowed mother take care of his younger siblings and was then ready to have a family of his own. Meanwhile, I assisted in giving care to my nephew whose parents were in America occupied with rearing twins and working to attain citizenship in America. He was asthmatic and needed constant care. At the same time, I also counseled and encouraged my father, who missed his wife, and my single adult brother, who felt lonely at the absence of our mother respectively.

At that time, my mother was working toward achieving permanent residency in the United States.

Eventually, we were all united in the United States of America as productive citizens. After forty-four years of marriage, my husband went home to be with the Lord in July of 2019. In retrospect, I see the hand of God who made all this possible and gave me the opportunity to serve Him through loving and taking care of my husband and extended family members when they needed me most. Like the Israelites, I was taught to honor and have faith in God who is powerful to make all our desires possible. God orchestrates the circumstances of our lives in order to fulfill His purpose which is always higher and better than we can imagine or plan. As children of God, we are endowed with spiritual insights which at times may not be quite clear, but if we persevere with patience, we see God's marvelous engineering.

Power of the Holy Spirit

The Spirit-filled person is now a child of God—COG—that means he/she may prosper, suffer, or be a miracle worker. All these possessions must be subject to the order of God's law where our parent God is worshipped and glorified, and the cue is taken from *big brother*, Jesus. Some prosper with material wealth, wisdom, and knowledge. This wealth must be employed in service to God, our parent; it must never be hoarded.

Some are called to endure suffering and discomfort and, this like wealth, must herald the parent God, giving Him glory and following the example of elder brother Jesus who suffered on the cross. So believers may suffer for God's glory. Suffering encourages as well as witnesses to those who will eventually suffer. Such witness expands the kingdom of God by those who will follow in similar fate. History bears evidence of how the church spread under persecution. "The blood of the martyrs is the seed of the Church."[4] Tertullian corroborated the power of Christian persecution and punishment that enhanced and enlarged the kingdom.

It is imperative for all born-again Christians to strive to develop spiritual acumen, and the best character trait to

---

[4] Tertullian was an early Christian apologist from North Africa and a renowned theologian.

acquire this exercise is discipline. Discipline, originating from the divine nature, subjects the human nature into conformity as disciples of Christ. It empowers human nature to acquire wisdom, strength, and insight necessary to withstand temptation and to achieve goals in service to God. For example, Jesus was in demand by the crowds who witnessed and experienced His healing powers, the miracles of food supplies, and His teachings. Yet Jesus called "time-out" in order for Him and His disciples to enjoy rest and relaxation necessary for the body. Discipline inspires human nature to express faith, thus witnessing to God's power. When faith is present, possibilities become realities, thus eradicating impossibilities. Therefore, faith is fully necessary to live as children of God and supports the chief pillar of the kingdom of God. The kingdom cannot exist without it.

Jesus displayed spiritual acumen when He spent an entire night praying on a mountain and on the next day, under the guidance of the Holy Spirit, selected the twelve apostles who became His constant companions (Luke 6:12–13). It was under this same Spirit's power that Jesus gave instructions on blessings and woes and established the command for Christians to love their enemies and to desist from judging one another, and taught what is known as the golden rule: to treat others as one expects to be treated (Luke 6:31). Meditation sharpens and enlightens the mind as a source of vision to discern the instructions of God and, in turn, infuse human nature with the faith to act. Theologian Thomas Aquinas best describes this revelation of the mind as the "beatific vision," a vision of the mind fueled by the power of the Holy Spirit through faith that conceives things that are to be from things that are not (Aquinas 1964). I had a distinct experience of this when my family and I moved to Georgia in 1989 and bought our home. We did not have enough funds to buy a new car. My husband insisted on a new car, having heard many episodes of the expenditure on used car repairs. We used public transportation, but it soon became a challenge, especially on shopping days. One day I felt direct instructions to go to the carport and take up a position as if I was sitting in a car driving. At first, I thought it was ridiculous. But the promptings from within were real, and I obeyed. At that time, I hoped none of my neighbors were looking. They certainly would have thought I had gone out of my mind, but I held the position for a few minutes. In the next month, my husband announced that he was ready to purchase the car. In a few weeks, I was actually at the wheel, sitting in a new car. This faith vision is appropriately exhibited n Hebrews 11:20 where Isaac blessed Jacob and Esau with prosperity that was not yet a reality. Obedience to the promptings of the Spirit is powerful. The mind is the eye of the Spirit, and through the lenses of the mind, the born-again may see God's plan for the future and execute such plan by converting it into reality.

Yet Jesus admits that He did not know the time of the second coming, so believers too, although inspired, are limited in knowledge of God. In spite of this fact, we keep pressing on to acquire more of God regardless of the fact that certain aspects of God are incomprehensible, and that is why He is God. However, the kingdom is among us and in us, and the inspirited is challenged to assist in making

God's kingdom a reality on earth as it is in heaven. The Holy Spirit opens the eyes of the believer to see beyond the darkness and access the glorious light. This status is achieved with dedication, attentiveness, and obedience to God's Word. The believer grows daily, and his/her eyes experience clearer vision and a keener sense of hearing under the discipline of the Holy Spirit. "They make their way from height to height, God shows himself to them in Zion" (Psalm 84:7).

Others perform miracles of healing and restoration. This too must be done for the glory of the parent God. Miracles must be free of any monetary compensation. Miracles enlarge the kingdom as its recipients are grateful and give praise and glory to God, thus creating believers of all who hear and witness its power. In all these categories, the children of God serve the parent God and rejoices in whatever way God designates. The child of God is cognizant of his/her state at all times and must report to parent God for evaluation and accountability of actions comparable to the example of big brother Jesus. The task of each child of God is to expand the kingdom of parent God whose prosperity is inexhaustible and has no limits. Just as the stars of the heavens and the sand on the seashore are immeasurable, so are the opulence and power of God.

Jesus was tempted at one of the high points of His life, as He had recently received the Holy Spirit and was put to the test immediately (Matthew 4). Unlike our ancestors Adam and Eve, Jesus did not yield under the devil's pressure but emerged victorious and ready to reveal God's love to the world. One must stay true to the Word, and

God will send His angels to minister and strengthen the Christian who desires to learn and obey His will. Stepping ahead of the Holy Spirit may cause great harm to the born-again as a sheep that strays away from under the shepherd's care. Prayers and God's Word keep the believer in step with the Holy Spirit.

History bears evidences about the wake of destruction and ill will perpetrated by some who erroneously claim to be acting under the direction of the Holy Spirit's power but were not. Jesus never promoted violence, and this fact must be the standard bearer of the Christian creed. The Holy Spirit brings life and power, not death nor destruction. The Holy Spirit's commands are never contrary to Jesus'. As the Scripture states, "But the Comforter, which is the Holy Ghost, whom the Father will send in my name, he shall teach you all things, and bring all things to your remembrance, whatsoever I have said unto you" (John 14:26).

Paul teaches that the Holy Spirit invades the believer so that one's body is considered the temple of God. The believer lives for Christ and no other, not even for oneself (1 Corinthians 6:19). The Holy Spirit guides, teaches, leads, protects, counsels, and grants wisdom, to name a few. When one is sensitive to this presence, one is elevated to do good works, to overcome evil, and to produce fruits acceptable to God. Similarly, as Christ performed miracles of healing and restoration, likewise the inspired believer is capable of doing the same. And as Jesus promised, that follower of Christ would do greater works than Him. Herein lies the great exchange since Christ returned to heaven with a glorified human body, which bears the marks of His suffering as our great high priest. It is therefore logical for the Holy Spirit to come down to earth. Jesus stated that unless He returns to the Father, the Holy Spirit cannot come (John 16:7).

Being born-again ushers the Christian into a new family—the divine holy family of God the Father, God the Son, and God the Holy Spirit. Jesus is conveying to Nicodemus that possessing the divine birthright prompts new sight, new possessions, new inheritance, new status, and a very new level of intelligence that endows the disciple of Christ to express faith and convert such faith into powerful actions. Being born-again into the divine holy family demands discipline, holiness, humility, confidence, and power for the disciple who must be ready to receive many wonderful things that God provides for His children. Faith allows Christians to tap into the kingdom and ask for what is desired or necessary to support his/her actions. The Holy Spirit would help the Christian to desire that which is in accordance with God the Father's manifesto.

There will be times when, as a born-again disciple, one will experience times of drought when the Holy Spirit seems distant. Nevertheless, take courage. God never abandons His followers. This may be considered a period of testing—a time in which one should strengthen one's faith and consider this silence as a time of spiritual growth where the mind receives discipline through constant prayer and by studying the Word. Often during this time, the divine nature receives new visions and revelation for the benefit of the disciple and for kingdom building. In pursuing the passion of the spirit of Christ, the disciple will often experience misunderstanding, judgment, and criticism from the world and even associates.

On the other hand, the disciple should not avoid God by hiding under the pretense of busyness. It will be beneficial to remember that God, the Creator, is the *one* who created time, and His disciples need to let go of distractions, worry, and stress so that he/she worships God in time and at all times. Praise God in prime time, not in time when the disciple ekes out a few minutes at the end of one's day to present pressurized praises. In contrast, spending time with the author of time, the disciple becomes more productive, efficient, and appreciative of the time ascribed. For God is the "I AM," the forever presence in life on this sphere and in the life to come. God transcends all time; He dwells in the absence of time—eternity. In grammar, "I am" is the first-person singular and represents the present tense of the verb "to be." The past, the present, and the future are the same to God who dwells in the absence of time which is always the present. Who does not like a present? Let the disciple accept and worship the present who saves and gives each one the abundant life.

The Holy Spirit is the manifestation of Jesus' presence in those who are born again so that He may continue to demonstrate his love and power to the world. We must never forget that we are witnesses of the love of Christ through whom God reveals Himself. Let no one be deceived or misconstrue the power of the Holy Spirit. It is important to remember that sinning against the Holy Spirit is unforgivable. "But whosoever speaketh against the Holy Ghost, it shall not be forgiven him, neither in this world, neither in the world to come; the consequence is eternal" (Mark 3:29).

For the born-again disciple, God holds the title of dual parenthood—God being the mother of creation (our humanity) and the father of the spiritual nature (our divinity). When the born-again offer up prayers of thanksgiving in joyful times, then it is natural to appeal to God in testing times. The same God who furnished the joy is capable of comforting the troubled mind. From each testing and trial, the Spirit-filled disciple can measure his/her spiritual progress by the success of the test. This test, formerly handled under human nature, conjures up a sense of regret and shame and propels the disciple to repentance of those actions of darkness. Self-examination allows the disciple to measure the distance he/she has traveled out of darkness into the marvelous spiritual light of the Spirit-filled world.

The study of the Bible promotes spiritual maturity, which leads to faith. Do not compromise the power of the Holy Spirit and His righteousness with the will of human nature and its lust. The disciple must allow the Spirit to extend His authority over the flesh. Decrease of the human nature's influence in the life of the born-again gives way to the increase and inspiration of the abundant life of the Holy Spirit. The born-again does well to remember that his/her spiritual progress supplies the ability to be a witness for Christ. Never leave the position as a witness of God's love to the world; it is the disciple's chief and bounded duty. Remember that a witness for Christ may take the form of faith, words, and actions.

Peter, before the power of the indwelling Holy Spirit, boasted on the premise of his human nature to die with Jesus and failed when identified by a high priest's maid of being one of the disciples. He denied that he knew Jesus, not once but thrice. This very disciple, born-again at Pentecost, healed the lame man in the temple and stood up in allegiance to Jesus against the rulers and religious leaders who objected to his righteous works of love and restoration (Acts 4:8–12). Taking stock of our status as born-again believers, what works of love and compassion have we accomplished, or are accomplishing on behalf of our spiritual Father?

The Holy Spirit generates power, love, and intelligence, which eliminate fear. The Scripture bears witness when Paul informs Timothy, "God has not given us the spirit of fear, but of power, and of love, and of a sound mind" (2 Timothy 1:7). The Holy Spirit's power casts away fear and promotes peace and builds faith and confidence. So much so that the writer of Hebrews invites Christians to approach the throne of grace boldly (Hebrews 4:16). History corroborates this boldness demonstrated by many of the early Christians who willingly faced martyrdom, rather than worship the emperor. I think those who suffered reasoned that their bodies were as good as dead because of sin and that the Spirit who possesses life was, by far, superior to their frail bodies that lie under the curse of destruction.

Over time and spiritual maturity, my outlook in life changed radically. I once was fearful of being disappointed and subsequently developed a negative spirit. As a student, when I was tested to make a sentence with a new word,

I often crafted a negative sentence. I entered most situations not expecting the highest or the best. For example, when standing in a queue for some free giveaway, I often anticipated that when it became my turn, the item would be exhausted, or a substitute would be given in its place. Often, the result was just as I had thought, and I would feel robbed or disheartened and wallow in a pity party.

However, since maturing in the Spirit as a child of God, I realized that pity parties demonstrate a lack of faith and trust in God to supply all my needs. They rob a believer of the abundant life Jesus came to give. It is not necessary for me to be disappointed when Christ is in charge. I have learned to leave everything to God, and even if I did not receive what I expected, I know that God has something much better for me. I have learned to trust God that disappointments are the beginning of divine appointments for higher or safer purposes.

Even in the event that a wonderful opportunity is thwarted, God has the omnipotence to offer the best alternative, and He does. We most often have to exercise patience in waiting. Therefore, I understand what Paul meant in Romans 8:28: "We know that all things work for good for those who love God, who are called according to his purpose." Note, Paul wrote "all things"; he did not say "some things," but "all things." With God on our side, the child of God is never disappointed but remains hopeful.

I recall that after graduating from high school, most of my friends found jobs that, as customary in my country, would eventually turn into lifelong careers. There was not much opportunity for work outside the traditional jobs in the public service, teaching or the military (police or the armed service). The opportunities were slim, and often, many applications would be turned down. I was feeling depressed, but I turned to prayers. One night, I attended a Pentecostal church meeting. It was not the church the family regularly attended, but my siblings and I would occasionally visit their evening service. On one such occasion, the pastor challenged the members to give generously, very generously. I had a small savings account which I had accumulated over a period of time, and I decided to take the pastor's challenge. The next week, I decided to give all that I had, although a voice deep within me tempted me to keep back a part of it. The temptation was real, but I adhered to the pastor's plea and gave my entire stash. Two weeks later, a well-known friend of my father who held a senior position in the public service called and offered me a position as a stenographer. That office was none other than the office of the prime minister, the highest office in the service.

This position was like a dream come true and led to many experiences, the chance to further my career and the opportunity to meet many world leaders and prime ministers. My extended family and friends were amazed at my fortune. Eventually, I was promoted, and through this position, I was instrumental in helping family and friends attain their ambitions. Two years later, I was introduced to the new personnel officer of the department who eventually became my husband. Because of this experience, I have matured spiritually and have learned to exercise faith in God and to develop the virtue of patience.

Miracles

We must allow the Holy Spirit to take the lead, always ahead of our carnal nature, which often rationalizes His orders, thus dishonoring His authority. This causes well-meaning believers to stumble in doubt and disobedience. The inspiritation means that the Holy Spirit occupies the Christian's entire being; no part of his/her body is inaccessible to the spiritual presence. Partial spiritual occupancy is not an option. Each day must be an experience to relate to His presence whether in thoughts, worship, work, deeds, hobbies, and special interests. We often refer to the workings of the Holy Spirit as coincidence while some refer to this as "God-incidence." One may have a need, and with the least effort on his/her part, that need is supplied by a stranger, an acquaintance, a friend, or a relative. On many occasions, I may be puzzled about the true meaning of a scripture, and when I happen to turn on the airwaves, a preacher explains the very verse I was contemplating. These are examples of the Holy Spirit at work in our lives.

There is a propensity for one to misuse the Holy Spirit's power, and this is heightened under the devil's guise to extend the temptation he initiated in the garden of Eden through one's thoughts. In an effort to thwart God's plan, he may attack the new born-again almost immediately. When the Christian succumbs to temptation, he/she reflects a distorted vision of the Holy Spirit and, as a result, causes great harm and confusion. Remember how at Jesus' baptism, the Holy Spirit descended on Him in the form of a dove as recorded in Luke 3:22. It is imperative that the Christian imitate Jesus, when shortly after His baptism in the River Jordan, He was tempted by the devil in the wilderness but remained resolute.

Those who believe in Christ are under the new birth and must cast off those habits of the human nature, which profit us nothing and are contrary to God's law. However, the new born-again are not exempt from trials, tribulations, and torment but rely on God for strength and vindication not necessarily in this world but definitely in the world to come. Like a baby learning to walk, new spiritual birthers may stumble and fall. But do not despair; God will not leave us but would offer His hand to save us and place us back in a right relationship with Him. Like Elijah, one must listen and heed the instructions of that divine silence (1 Kings 19:12).

Progress is attained when the disciple's vision, captured in the realm of human imagination, now expands into heights of spiritual shrewdness. This new panoramic vision assists the Christian to acquire spiritual gifts far different from the earthly gifts that promoted personal pursuits and selfish gain. The spiritual gifts, unlike the earthly talents that are often stacked away or ignored, compels the Christian to employ them for the glory of the divine family. Therefore, this fact validates what Jesus said, "The Advocate, the holy Spirit that the Father will send in my name—he will teach you everything and remind you of all that I told you" (John 14:26). As a result, the divine nature, not left to wander without purpose, takes the cue from the Holy Spirit. Spiritual gifts emblazoned in selfless love promotes the enlargement of the spiritual family and advancement of God's kingdom.

In addition, being born-again means also being ready to endure trials, tribulations, and other adverse conditions in life. Conditions that, without the help of the Spirit, will be impossible to bear or endure. These adversities demand discipline and spiritual maturity that witnesses to the story of Job who, in spite of his righteousness, experienced the loss of his earthly family and possessions. Spiritual vision commandeers the human nature to rise above its concerns and focus on faith in the Father to supply the strength necessary to endure. Such spiritual insight caused Job to declare, "As for me, I know that my vindicator lives, and that he will at last stand forth upon the dust. This will happen when my skin has been stripped off, and from my flesh I will see God" (Job 19:25). This example corroborates the demands by Jesus for the disciple to exercise faith and take up his/her cross and follow Him. Many pilgrims, past and present, experienced and will experience the burden of the cross which often leads to death but, like Jesus, will rise to eternal life.

God is benevolent. This is evidenced in the fact that we mortals have the ability to question God and to debate about our existence. This proves that God is merciful in decreeing the nature of free will to humans, thus granting us the ability to analyze and choose the blessing or the curse.

The Holy Spirit teaches us the Word of God, and God interprets its meaning for our lives and grants the ability to instruct others. Therefore, it is imperative that Christians read and study the books of the Bible. This should be a daily routine as food is a daily regimen for the physical well-being, so God's Word feeds the Spirit and develops our divine nature. This is what Jesus meant when He declared, "It is written, that man shall not live by bread alone, but by every word of God" (Luke 4:4). The Word of God is inexhaustible. The counsel of the Holy Spirit interprets the Word of God and contributes to the discipline and development of our divine nature in order to assist us in our maturity. This relationship of the Holy Spirit to the apostles captured by Christopher Ash states, "It is that the process of learning will take a lifetime and therefore will need a lifetime tutor as they—as it were—work through the revelation of the Father in Jesus" (*Hearing the Spirit*, page 60). Therefore, the Holy Spirit nourishes and flourishes the disciple of Christ, blazing a path of service here and for eternity. This service, indelibly ingrained in the sands of time, emboldens present and future pilgrims.

There is enough for kingdom building. It is difficult for the child of God to realize the prosperity of his/her parent God because scarcity and lack, while a reality in the natural arena, are not part of God's persona. Therefore, we children of God are equally equipped to enjoy and helpfully distribute the prosperity and blessings of parent God. We must never neglect to acknowledge and give praise to

God. Children of God have no fear, no lack, no wants, no limits or inaccessibility to *parent* God since they are reborn by water and the blood. They belong and are in the family of parent God the Father, God the Son, and God the Holy Spirit. In this new relationship, children of God are not just humanly begotten; they are spiritually begotten.

To be born from above is to be born under the divine nature in contrast to the human nature that is earthly. These natures are not opposed to each other, and the elements of water is common to both natures. The physiological birth of a baby does include water, which signals that the baby is about to enter the world. Jesus informed Nicodemus of being born by water that refers to the Holy Spirit—God. Thus, water serves as the common factor signaling the birth of both the human and divine natures—the divine as in the waters of baptism.

The kingdom of God consists of two facades that is similar to our dual nature. One consists of its presence here on earth, and the other part exists above—the outer world. The kingdom on earth is present in divine order, peace, healing, serving, sharing, and caring. Jesus describes this kingdom to the disciples of John the Baptist, "Go and tell John what you have seen and heard: the blind regain their sight, the lame walk, lepers are cleansed..." (Luke 7:22). The Messiah has ushered in the kingdom of God on earth.

Likewise, in imitating Jesus, the born-again disciple uses faith to achieve peace, wisdom, knowledge, talents, understanding, caring, compassion, healing, and prayers as foundation blocks for establishing God's kingdom on earth. The weapon of faith wages wars and conquers doubt, limitation, lack, need, spiritual blindness, poverty, sickness, etc. I have realized the true meaning of Jesus' declaration: "But without faith it is impossible to please him..." (Hebrews 11:6). Faith is the key that taps into God's power, thus enabling the Spirit-filled believer to accomplish miracles for God's glory and grace. Faith grants spiritual vision to experience the limitless kingdom of God and overcomes the limits of the earthly kingdom.

The kingdom above is where God abides—heaven. It is vast and beyond what the human mind is capable of determining; lack nor boundaries exist there. For the kingdom of God exists without the constraints of time but operates in possibilities. The apostle Paul who had a glimpse of this realm when he "was caught up" in the Spirit stated that it was impossible to repeat and describe what he heard and saw respectively (2 Corinthians 12:2). However, only faith, which the born-again must exercise in order to accesses the possibilities of this kingdom of God can convert its incredible principles into reality. When this is accomplished, miracles happen, God's kingdom comes to earth, and, in that moment of time, God-incidence occurs.

For example, numbers diverge in value under the Spirit's directive where five barley loaves and two small fishes were adequate to feed five thousand people with twelve baskets of fragments remaining (John 6). Significantly, the number of elements used in this miracle is seven (five plus two), a number which denotes completion or sufficiency. In addition, Jesus' resurrection establishes hope for all God's children. After suffering cruelly on the Roman cross where He died, Jesus resurrects bodily on the third day, leaving his tomb empty and proving that God has overcome death and the grave. The possibility of life comes out of the darkest hour in human history.

Thus, faith opens the door to a grand kingdom life. Grand in the sense that it encompasses all possibilities, fair or unfair, peace or turmoil, providence or scarcity, safety or dangers, rich or poor, weak or strong, defense or vulnerable, in sickness or in health. And the list continues. The disciple may encounter some or all the above, but this should not deter him/her because God is present and will be present in all of situations. God transforms the possible negatives into possible positives. The born-again must always consider possibilities because it is the pillars of the kingdom of God. As the Scripture points out, "But with God all things are possible" (Matthew 19:26). To the disciple who understands this concept, the sky is not the limit; the possibilities are endless as is reminiscent with God's kingdom. Abraham believed God's promise to raise up descendants as numberless as the stars when he was yet childless, and God considered his faith as righteous (Genesis 15:6). A fulfillment is visible to this present day, for Abraham is known as the "father of all nations."

God's Passover commandment obtained the release of the Israelites from bondage in Egypt to freedom in the promised land. By the power of God, they passed through the Red Sea on dry land, a sign of baptism. This Passover lamb was a precursor to Christ, who gave His life on the cross as the ultimate Passover and who gifted the life of the Spirit to the born-again by His glorious resurrection from the dead. The Scripture records that blood and water flowed from Jesus' side from the wound perpetrated by a Roman soldier (John 19:34). By awesome means, the blood of Jesus obtained liberty from slavery to sin for all who believe in the abundant life of His kingdom. Note the elements of water and blood present in the natural birth also form part of the new birth. The Holy Spirit decrees freedom to believers who dwell in the kingdom of God.

God, in His great love, has made it possible for humans to be born again and to receive an inheritance that is imperishable through the resurrection of His beloved Son, Jesus Christ. Without being born again, one is partially alive. God's Passover commandment in Egypt saved the lives of the Israelites and obtained their release from bondage to freedom in the land of Canaan, promised to Abraham. The Passover lamb was a shadow of Jesus, who gave His life on the cross as the ultimate Passover and who brought the presence of the Spirit so that the disciple who possesses him is passed from slavery to sin to become an inheritor of the kingdom life. Jesus' blood atones for and covers the sin of the born-again. This fact resonates in the Scripture when the soldiers were unable to divide Jesus' garment because it was seamless—woven from top to bottom (John 19:23). The design of Jesus' robe indicates the complete cover of sin. His robe was designed with no openings or seams from which sin can seep; for Jesus' tunic has metaphorically covered the sin of all who follow Him.

Spiritual Maturity

In the loneliness of life when no one is there to help or comfort the disciple, one must remember that God through the Holy Spirit will never leave or abandon the disciple. God is present, strengthening the disciple and pouring out wisdom in the valley of lonesomeness. Jesus experienced abandonment so that His followers may enjoy the presence of God at all times (2 Timothy 4:17).

This new birth may conflict with one's relationship, especially in cases with family and the social circle of friends who do not know Christ. One may have to choose, and though it may be difficult, the best choice is obviously the spiritual family for whom Jesus, our Savior, has won for us through His death and resurrection. The solution is to pray for the salvation of the natural family members who object to your membership in the new spiritual family of God. This situation clarifies and gives meaning to the declaration made by Jesus: "If anyone comes to me and does not hate his own father and mother and wife and children and brothers and sisters, yes, and even his own life, he cannot be my disciple" (Luke 14: 26). I knew of a co-worker who had emigrated from India and related how his father was totally opposed to his becoming a Christian and threatened to kill him.

The tension between the divine and human natures was captured in Jesus' agony in the Garden of Gethsemane, where He fell to the ground and cried to God, "Abba Father, all things are possible to you. Take this cup away from me, but not what I will but what you will" (Mark 14:36). Jesus' divine nature eventually triumphed over the flesh when He succumbed to His Father's will. In contrast, Peter who had not yet received the Holy Spirit surrendered under pressure to his human nature in denying his master, even though he had originally pledged his loyalty to Him (Mark 14:31).

All born-again Christians must strive to develop their spiritual acumen, and the best character trait to acquire this exercise is discipline. Discipline, while elevating the divine nature, subjects the human nature to obedience. This obedience to discipline is necessary for this nature to submit to the divine, thus allowing the divine to have control and responsibility of behaviors and determine decisions. For example, Jesus was in demand by the crowd because of His healing powers and miracles of instant food supplies. But in spite of these demands, Jesus knew when to take time off. The Scripture bears record of the time He took off to pray, rest, and relax. After an extensive healing session, Jesus spent a night on a mountaintop in prayer. This fact demonstrates the necessity for the human nature to rest and recuperate in order for the divine nature to hear the communication of the Holy Spirit concerning new directives.

The study of the Bible promotes spiritual maturity, which leads to faith. Do not compromise the power of the Holy Spirit and His righteousness with the will of human nature and its lust. The disciple must allow the Spirit to extend His authority over the flesh. Decrease of the human nature's influence in the life of the born-again gives way to the increase and inspiration of the abundant life of the Holy Spirit. The born-again does well to remember that his/her spiritual progress supplies the ability to be a witness for Christ. Never leave the post as witness of God's love to the world; it is the disciple's chief and bounded duty. Remember that a witness for Christ may take the form of faith, words, and actions. Do not refrigerate faith; frozen faith is useless. Faith must be active and at the ready for its engagement and application.

Evidence of the Trinity is abundant both in the Old and the New Testaments. In the beginning, God visited Adam and Eve in their Eden home. The Holy Trinity appeared to Abraham at noonday at the Oak of Mamre in the form of three men who brought good news of Sarah's future child, Isaac, and pronounced the impending doom of Sodom and Gomorrah (Genesis 18). The prefigured Jesus appeared to Jacob during the night and wrestled with him when the wrestler dislocated Jacob's hip but blessed him (Genesis 32:25–29). God revealed to Samson's mother that she must drink no wine even before his birth and after he was born. Samson was known for his exceptional strength (Judges 13:8). God appeared to Moses in the burning bush at the foot of Mount Sinai and gave instructions for delivering the Israelites from slave labor in Egypt (Genesis 3:2). God appeared to Paul, on the Road to Damascus, as a bright light and instructed him on the procedure for becoming an apostle (Acts 9).

The Christian life ought to be supernatural as the Holy Spirit sharpens our ears and opens our eyes to see Him and adjust our hearts to obey His commands. The Spirit-filled Christian reflects the life of Jesus like a body of water which mirrors its surrounding scenery. The Christian strives to become like Jesus with both natures of divinity and humanity cooperating in a wonderful display of unity and fortitude to perform miracles, to console, to labor, to visit the sick, to bring the good news of the gospel to those who are lost. The divine nature must lift us up above the natural realm and take us by faith to the realm of possibilities and for us to witness beatific visions, like feeding the multitude of our day with five barley loaves and two fish.

Christians should all be Oscar winners—not that we work toward gaining this momentary, temporary trophy but an eternal, incorruptible trophy God is preparing for all those who have obeyed His commands. Christians are all actors as we seek to imitate the actions and mercies displayed by Jesus who came down to earth to dwell among us and who left a sterling example of what is required of us who follow His commandments and show forth His mercies. The nature of God should always be present in the life of the Christian, ever seeking new ways to enhance our service and elevate the lives of our brothers and sisters who have eyes to see yet are blind.

Operating under the influence of the Holy Spirit may compare the believer's life to organic foods. Organic foods are rich with natural nutrients. In contrast, lab-enhanced substitutes may lack food value yet appeal to our senses. The inspired person is reborn to a purpose-driven life that invigorates not only one's life but also the lives of those whom he/she encounters.

Therefore, we must claim the Holy Spirit who gives us the opportunity to exist beyond the natural limitations and become part of the family of God—the Holy Trinity. Rev. Holt explains this position in describing the process of baptism. He teaches, "When a new member is presented to the congregation, we will leave off his family of origin name. This is because, no matter which earthly family he or she belongs to, the newly baptized person is also getting a new family, the family of God, and is being adopted as a spiritual child of God" (Holt 2015).[5] The human nature must cooperate with the divine nature, the corruptible under the mandate of the incorruptible. For faith is the engine that propels the divine nature that seeks to execute the commands of the Spirit. Thus, these dual natures capture the essence of the whole person unified in obedience to God and in service to humankind.

In maintaining a healthy relationship with the Holy Spirit, one must meditate on the Word of God—the Bible—and invite family members, neighbors, and even total strangers to do the same. In studying the Word, love flourishes, and selfish ambition diminishes because love points to its original connection, God our Father. Thus, it deems necessary to evaluate the connective power from time to time, ensuring that it is safe and free from entanglements, such as personal elements of self-indulgent and carnal cravings of human nature. Inspiritation is the igni-

---

[5] Charlie Holt, *The Crucified Life: Seven Words from the Cross,* day 17, page 93.

tion that influences the power of inspiration. This fact manifested magnificently on the day of Pentecost when Peter defended and explained the arrival of the Holy Spirit against the critical thoughts of the people present concerning this phenomenon. Peter's clarification resulted in the birth of the church (Acts 2).

Through the blood of Jesus, Christians are adopted into the family of God—a family where Jesus is the *firstborn*, and believers are siblings of Jesus. Now, since the firstborn Jesus is comprised of the divine and human natures, Christians who are His siblings must be clothed in the same dual nature. The fact is that it was necessary for Jesus who is Spirit to become human, and in similar fashion, the Christian who is human (carnal) must put on spirituality to be like Jesus, both divine and human. This is not blasphemous as some may be inclined to think because Jesus made this prerequisite when He instructed Nicodemus that he must be born from above (John 3:7).

The above means by the Holy Spirit, the *third* being of the Godhead who takes up residence within the body of the Christian, transforming the body into the temple of God. This is identical to the incarnate nature of Jesus Christ, the firstborn. Since Jesus is referred to as the firstborn, subsequently He must have other siblings. These are those who have come to believe in Him—those born-again. Christians are no longer slaves to sin (under the mastery of human nature) but children of God and joint heirs with Christ (Titus 3:7). Paul in Romans chapter 8 captures the essence of this new status of Jesus being big brother to all those who are born-again. "For those he foreknew he also predestined to be conformed to the image of his Son, so that he might be the firstborn among many brothers" (Romans 8:29). Of course, Paul is writing in the period of gender insensitivity, hence the word "brothers," which includes sisters as well.

After Jesus is resurrected and ascended up to heaven, God exchanges Jesus' mortal presence and replaces Him with the Holy Spirit whose composite is powerful to indwell every Christian with the possibility of expressing the power of Jesus' divinity through our human nature, hence the phrase "born again." The indwelling of the Holy Spirit engineers a new birth, not just a different relationship but also a remaking of each person, linking us to the family of the Godhead with Jesus as our oldest *sibling*. Remember the conversation Jesus had with Nicodemus in John 3, instructing this Jewish leader that he must be born again. Jesus supports this new relationship of family because He uses the word "brothers," not "disciples," when He assigned Mary to convey to His frightened disciples the glorious message of His resurrection.

Jesus, after His resurrection, teaches Mary Magdalene that His followers' relationship with Him is now changed to a spiritual one when He instructed Mary not to touch Him as He had not yet returned to His Father (John 20:17). Therefore, Christians must develop their faith as we learn to relate to God through the Holy Spirit. After Jesus' return to the Father—and I am sure, with heavenly fanfare, glorification, and rejoicing—the Holy Spirit was sent to indwell every believer with the new person of Jesus—the divine nature. In Jesus' pre-resurrection state, it would have been impossible for each believer to share His presence simultaneously. The Holy Spirit makes possible the power of Jesus' divinity to dwell alongside our human nature. This is the new birth for all who believe, not just a different relationship with God but a remaking of each believer. He elevates the new relationship of every Christian to one of being within the family of God.

Ezekiel's vision of the water flowing through the temple corroborates the conversation Jesus had with the Samaritan woman at the well. Jesus told her that she should have asked Him and He would have given her "living water." For the water she sought at the well is inadequate to quench her thirst, but the water He will provide consists of an eternal flow. Jesus described it: "But whoever drinks the water I shall give will never thirst; the water I shall give will become in him a spring of water welling up to eternal life" (John 4:14). Water represents the Holy Spirit's presence and inexhaustible power to transform the believer into an awe-inspiring witness for Christ in the world. However, one must work at the development and not sit idly by as Paul advised in the Thessalonians: "Do not quench the Spirit" (1 Thessalonians 5:19). It is possible to be spiritually lethargic, which stifles one's work for the Lord. In this state of spiritual lethargy, the fruits are negatively affected and, at the final judgment, will be found deficient. Therefore, one needs to be watchful, ever efficient in the presence of the Spirit and His work that God will eventually judge.

The Holy Spirit empowers the born-again with the revelation of God's kingdom. The earthly nature is constrained to envision God's kingdom. Because human nature sees limits, boundaries, and capacities as is pertinent to itself while God's kingdom has no limits, borders, or measurements and is, in a word, wider than human imagination. To experience such requires spiritual insight, not mere vision but the empowerment of the mind—the mind of Christ.

In analyzing Jesus' response to Nicodemus's statement about recognizing that He came from God, Jesus declared that no one could see the kingdom of God without being born again. Jesus' answer reveals that flesh and blood—our humanity—is unable to live in the realm of timelessness. Human nature, confined by time and place, is limited, but the Spirit of God lives beyond the realm of time. He dwells in the absence of time—eternity. This is why Jesus' response to the dilemma is new birth. If we, as disciples, relate to Christ and enjoin the family of God, then it behooves us to acquire the divine nature. This revelation is manifested at the time of Peter's confession as to who Jesus is and Jesus' declaration that this information could not come from Peter's intellectual ability (human nature) but from a divine revelation from God the Father (Matthew 16:16–18). It is impossible for human nature to ascertain the things of the Spirit. Paul also supports this fact in his letter to the church at Galatia that, in preparation for his mission to the Gentiles, he did not seek the wisdom of human nature, those who were apostles before him, but retreated to Arabia in pursuit of spiritual counsel (Galatians 1:16).

Jesus, as mentioned in the Scripture, went to bring the good news to those who had gone before, as in the time of Noah when, through disbelief, they all perished, except for Noah and his family. According to 1 Peter 3, Jesus spent the time between His death and His resurrection ministering to those who had perished, giving them another opportunity to choose the abundant life God had originally planned for humankind. For this reason, many churches today recite the Apostles' Creed, reiterating this fact, "He [Jesus] suffered under Pontius Pilate, was crucified, died and was buried. He descended to the dead. The third day he rose again." (Book of Common Prayer).

God revealed our two-part nature when He prophesied to Abraham of his forthcoming demise. God explained that Abraham would join his ancestors in peace, referring to Abraham's divine nature, the Spirit, and that his body, human nature, would be buried at a happy old age (Genesis 15:14). This is how Jesus explained to the Jews that Abraham saw His day, which is the period of Jesus on earth, and rejoiced. Thus, indicating that Abraham's divine nature is alive and well (John 8:56).

However, the Holy Spirit living in the Christian produces power, but that power must stay connected to the source—Christ. The maintenance of the connection is crucial to the effectiveness of the power since any disconnection diffuses power and creates chaos, confusion, conceit, havoc, misunderstanding, and false directives. This situation often transforms inwardly to one's self-aggrandizement with increasing thirst to become the center of the universe. A center based on narcissism attracting the feeble of mind, the weak, and the unsuspecting masses that through history has resulted in cults of various phantasms leading to dissolution and death.

The kingdom of God rests in the mind. Until one is filled with the Spirit, one's mind is confined to the earth realm—human nature. On the other hand, when one is born of the Spirit, one has insight into God's illustrious kingdom which is beyond the scope of human vision. Believers must grow and practice to stretch their minds to a level far beyond what they are accustomed to in the natural realm. The spiritual arena is awesome as God is awesome and the Holy Spirit. With a steady dose of the Word (spiritual food), the born-again may develop this new sight which alters one's life completely. This is the purpose for the scriptural declaration that anyone who accepts Christ is a new creation. Old things have passed; behold, all things become new. Children of God, rise up and access the kingdom with all your new mind. The kingdom of God has no limits, no borders, no time, no distance, no constraints of the good, no evil. The kingdom of God is fortified by grace.

In contrast, the good of the natural realm is under time and thus subject to destruction. The party comes to an end, and everyone leaves for one reason or another. Human nature, tarnished by sin, is immature and feeble; it is half alive and thus under the curse of corruption. The laws of nature are under the clock, and the law which when transgressed produces death. The natural world is beautiful because God created all of it, but because of sin, it lacks the full potential of its original purpose. Nevertheless, all is not lost. God will return to reinstate it one day to its original status. In the meanwhile, God offers His followers spiritual sight and the opportunity to become a part of His king-dom which permeates the earthly and the heavenly spheres.

This is what Jesus meant in his conversation with Nicodemus. Without the Holy Spirit, we are shortsighted and spiritually handicapped. There is no bargain to be struck under the human nature. Jesus, in the conversation with this Jewish leader, issues an imperative: "Amen, Amen I say to you, no one can enter the kingdom of God without being born of water and Spirit" (John 3:5). The born-again enters the kingdom of God by the power of thought, not by a 747 jet airplane, a spacecraft, or a satellite but by spiritual sight fueled by faith. The body needs not travel to a specific place but, through the power of the mind, attains access to the kingdom—the mind serving as the travel module. Hence, we pray, "Thy kingdom come, thy will be done in earth as it is in heaven." Jesus discusses this fact when He related, "Amen, I say to you, if you have faith the size of a mustard seed, you will say to this mountain, move from here to there, and it will move (Matthew 17:20).

Suffering and Obedience

The disciple is no longer destitute, wayward, hungry, homeless, naked, mistreated, and abused through the power of sin, the devil, and the flesh. He/she is adopted into the family of God with all the rights and privileges of a true heir, "because those who are led by the Spirit of God are sons of God...but you received the Spirit of sonship. And by him we cry Abba, Father. The Spirit himself testifies with our spirit that we are God's children" (Romans 8:14–16). Yet this new status of the Spirit-filled life of a disciple develops a humble spirit, in total obedience to God. The disciple must be prepared and willing to share in the suffering of Christ our Lord because we are now in the family. We are never to despair because the Scripture informs us that our omnipotent Father maneuvers the evil circumstance that malign us to work for our good (Romans 8:28).

One must be prepared to participate in the suffering of Christ so that there is now one family united in purpose by suffering as our elder brother Jesus did. As our elder brother, Jesus suffered to procure our salvation and elevation to the spiritual family of God. Hence, as His disciples, we too must share in suffering in order to bring glory to God. It is not just that we suffer but the way in which the born-again goes through it is on full display. However, this spiritual family—the church—will eventually move on to enjoy eternal joy and freedom in the region of timelessness (Romans 8:17). Just as in a typical family where each member shares the household chores, the Christian identifies as a member of God's spiritual household and accepts the lot dealt him/her.

In some assemblies, proof of the Holy Spirit's presence in a disciple is often portrayed as a charismatic experience that is expected and serves as proof that the disciple is born-again. The ability of speaking in a foreign language (the gift of tongues) was the hallmark of the early church. In certain denominations, it serves as legitimate admittance to the fellowship of its members. While these enigmatic states are acceptable, it should not rival the one of quiet contemplation and transformation through gradual growth. As Paul declared, "For I have learned, in whatsoever state I am, therewith to be content" (Philippians 4:11).

There should be no rivalry in the household of God, for each member possesses a unique contribution in the building up of this spiritual house. Paul's admonition of the early church concerning this spirit of rivalry is recorded in the Scripture and is appropriate for all times. "There are different kinds of spiritual gifts but the same Spirit: there are different forms of service, but the same Lord, there are different workings but the same God who produces all of them in everyone" (1 Corinthians 12:4). No one gift is superior to another because all spiritual gifts come from God, and all things from God are perfect and purpose driven. The manner of the manifestation of the Holy Spirit in each follower of Christ rests solely on God's prerogative in relation to time, place, and purpose. It is the responsibility of the believer to make use of this gift wisely, effectively, and efficiently, always keeping in mind the source of the gift—God Almighty.

Oswald Chambers states, "I am not a superior person among other people. I am a bondservant of the Lord Jesus" (Chambers 2000).[6] It is with this view that Christians develop the true relationship with God, a relationship enhanced by the Holy Spirit who teaches to listen and obey and to pray and not to fear. The Christian, empowered by the Holy Spirit, bears fruits in obedience to the works that God has delegated him/her to do. These works may vary according to the time and place in the present and in history, but behaviors and the code of conduct of the follower of Christ must be the same for one another and similar to the master. As taught by Christ in the Beatitudes, "blessed are the peacemakers for they shall be called the children of God" (Matthew 5:9). Therefore, it behooves all Christians to seek for peace and to pursue it. These codes of conduct distinguish the follower of Christ from those of the world. This is how the Christians in earlier times paved the way for Christianity to take its place and become known to the pagan world. Their witness also brought them much suffering and often death. Many, filled with the Holy Spirit, thought it a privilege to suffer humiliation for the sake of Christ. As were the apostles, "they departed from the coun-

---

[6] Oswald Chambers, *My Utmost for His Highest: Selections for the Year*, daily devotion, July 15.

cil, rejoicing that they were counted worthy to suffer shame for his name" (Acts 5:41).

Jesus ascended to heaven, and the Holy Spirit came down as Jesus promised on the day of Pentecost where all the disciples were gathered. The Holy Spirit gave Peter the power to rise up and defend his fellow apostles who were not drunk but being indwelt by the Holy Spirit. His speech on this glorious day caused about three thousand to become disciples of God, which led them to repentance and baptism—the beginning of the church (Acts 2). Peter instructed that they also will receive the Holy Spirit (Acts 2:38). The inspiritation of these new Christians changed their lives to that of devotion and commitment to the community. "They devoted themselves to the teaching of the apostles and to the communal life, to the breaking of the bread and to the prayers" (Acts 2:42). In the book of Acts, the evidence of the inspiritation—the new birth—is distinctly manifested among the early Christians and continues to this day. His power does not cease to amaze Christ's disciples. This should not be a surprise as Jesus spoke of the inspiritation while here on earth. He instructed his disciples, "But when he comes, the Spirit of truth, he will guide you to all truth" (John 16:13 CSB).

This Spirit of truth continues to infiltrate the lives of many, causing the expansion of the church in spite of culture, race, or ethnicity. It is the duty of every Christian to make disciples for Christ and to shine in the corner wherever that corner exists. The new birth empowers and strengthens the church to do the work of God. This work accomplishes the will of God through the varying gifts that the believer is endowed with by the Almighty God. The manifestation of the Holy Spirit is not for personal gain but to reveal God to the world because the believer is the medium through which Christ is made known. However, many are skeptical or wary concerning spiritual gifts, but these gifts may be tested by the fruits they bear.

The power of the rebirth is grossly underestimated by believers. Those who are reborn by the Spirit have the same power as Jesus Christ who was in humankind with us and healed, restored the depressed, forgave sins, and resurrected the dead. The born-again has Christ's power to perform the very miracles He did. However, this spiritual consciousness is not for the manifestation of human power and prestige but for the furtherance of God's kingdom. Those inspired by the Holy Spirit display the humility of Jesus which is upholding the commandments, praying constantly, and studying God's Word—the Bible. Pursuing these disciplines, the believer's acumen is powerfully enhanced and the senses are sharpened so that it becomes effortless to hear the voice of the Holy Spirit giving instructions from time to time.

Of course, obedience to the Holy Spirit's instructions is crucial to the development of this new birth in the Spirit. The call to obedience may not be extraordinary or exceptional but camouflaged in such simplicity that it is easily missed or ignored, and in this failure to comprehend and obey, the believer's progress is hindered. Thus, disobedience affects spiritual growth and stymies an in-depth relationship. However, in such times, one is given another chance to improve on the relationship by repenting.

Most often, it serves as a teaching point when the Spirit's instruction is repeated or presented in another form. In the episode of Naaman the Syrian general, a great warrior who was a leper, approached the prophet Elisha for healing. Elisha by the power of the Holy Spirit instructed him to have a bath in the Jordan River. Naaman became angry and thought the procedure insignificant. Nevertheless, one of his companions encouraged him to obey the prophet's command, stating, "My father, if the prophet told you to do something extraordinary, would you not do it?" (2 Kings 5:13). He finally obeyed and was healed. On the other hand, the Scripture bears record of an example of obedience to the instructions of God, the Holy Spirit. Abraham obeyed immediately after hearing God's directive to sacrifice Isaac, his beloved son. "Early the next morning Abraham saddled his donkey, took with him two of his servants and his son Isaac, and after cutting the wood for the burnt offering, set out for the place of which God had told him" (Genesis 22:3). However, God intervened and provided a ram as the sacrifice. As a result of his obedience, God blessed Abraham: "That because you acted as you did in not withholding from me your son, your only one, I will bless you…" (Genesis 22:16). Abraham was called the friend of God (James 2:23).

Christians ought to be disciplined in studying the Word and in improving relationships with the Holy Spirit. As one obeys the directive of the Holy Spirit, the more one becomes sensitive and alert to His prodding. This obedience achieves a high sense of the divine order regarding one's mission in answering the great commission. Of course, the flesh, our human nature, most often rebels or refuses to cooperate in compliance with His divine orders. Hence, by being conscious of this tug-of-war between our natures, we pray often and have the words of the Scripture etched in our memories and our minds to apply whenever necessary.

A wonderful experience Jesus left for us is His temptation in the wilderness after He was baptized and was fasting for forty days—when the devil temped Jesus to convert those brown loaflike-shaped terracotta stones to become bread. It was the first and most grueling temptation to satisfy the human nature, which was straining to be satiated. Jesus' divinity reminds believers that this nature must also be fed. Jesus' reply to Satan is revealing since it addresses the appetites of both natures (Matthew 4:4). Just as the body needs food, so the spiritual nature needs the Word of God. One does not supersede the other, but both are nourished so that the two natures become one in a seamless life.

The perfect example of this maturity of dual natures we glean from the Scripture that Jesus grew in wisdom and stature and gained the respect of God and humankind (Luke 2:52). This reveals that we as Christians must develop our spiritual acumen as well as our natural development. Our human nature is readily seen in our physical growth development where one moves from childhood to puberty and then adulthood. Our voices may change from the high-pitched innocence of a child to a lower, stronger base; muscles become visible during this transition. Both natures bear fruit. Likewise, as in the physical nature, many procreate as directed and designed by God to multiply and replenish the earth (Genesis 1:28). We exist as evidence of the sexuality of our parents and ancestors in accordance with God's commands.

Likewise, the development and growth of the Holy Spirit dwelling within reveals wise decisions in life's choices and the ability to bear worthy fruits of the Spirit. This spiritual growth is reflected in our countenance; there is a glow in the eyes of the person who experience the Spirit's council. The way believers operate and demonstrate spiritual fruits distinguishes the Christian life. Wisdom derives from the application of knowledge of God and His unconditional love. The love of God attests to the multitude of martyrs of the faith over the history of the church. Many early Christians willingly died for the faith.

The display of the fruit of the Holy Spirit is strictly to cause praise and glory to be given to God; it is not to be treated or honored as personal achievements or talents. All the praise and honor of the fruit of the Holy Spirit demonstrated in the world should stimulate people to praise and worship God and God alone (*sola gloria*). Dangerous consequences lurk in the shadows of persons accepting praise for the operation of these fruits. After such demonstration of the fruit of the Holy Spirit, one ought to be vigilant in pointing the compliments to God. Personally delighting in praise is robbing God of the glory due to His name and places one in the predicament of being worshipped—a scenario all too familiar in the church, which contributes to the demise of gifted Christian leaders and pastors in the community. Nevertheless, praise is acceptable and may serve as encouragement to the saint, and the saint, serving as conduit, allows praise to waft its way to God.

In the development of the relationship with the Holy Spirit, the recipient is convinced and believes, which leads to obedience and culminates into action. After one Thanksgiving celebration, I had much leftovers, and I received instruction from the Holy Spirit to make soup with the leftovers and take it to my church where sandwiches are distributed at a noontime lunch for the homeless community. I decided to obey and made a giant pot of turkey soup. It was more than welcomed when, on the cold day, I distributed it. The folks were surprised and grateful and complimented me on its deliciousness. I remembered saying thank you to their compliments as I was leaving, but on second thoughts, I immediately turned back and said, "To God be the glory." Then several of them repeated what I said, "To God be the glory." Obedience to the Holy Spirit made praises ascend to God that cold day.

The Holy Spirit is the presence of Jesus Christ dwelling within each believer, and since Jesus was incarnate, we as humans are made spiritual by His power. Believers relate to God through the Holy Spirit. This is why the Scripture states, "But the hour cometh, and now is, when the true worshippers shall worship the Father in spirit and in truth; for the Father seeketh such to worship him" (John 4:23). The inspiritation grants the power of Jesus to the believer and enables him/her to perform miracles of healing and restoration as well as counseling in order to witness to the love of Christ and His redeeming sacrifice as our great high priest. With the presence of the Holy Spirit living within each disciple, one may feel the exuberant nature of knowledge and understanding bursting out from the born-again disciple and ushering new possibilities for witnessing to God's glory and grace.

Those within the radius of the inspirited believer's influence are blessed by his/her spiritual power. For example, history teaches that hospitals owe their existence to Christians who created a way to care for the sick and helpless and those who were causalities of war. Schools were established by churches in an effort to educate the masses and enable them to read the Bible. As a matter of fact, the Bible was often the only textbook available; and the schools were managed by priests, pastors, and leading laity. Today, missionaries and college students seek innovative ways to reach out to people living in the remotest ends of the earth in order to alleviate hunger and to spread the gospel of Christ. These graduating young college students maneuver the technology to improve water supplies to villagers by digging wells and purifying the waters of rivers and streams. The born-again children of God contribute not only to the spiritual development of the populace but make significant contribution to civil administration in the community as well.

The Holy Spirit's presence in the Christian's life is the fulfillment of Jesus' promise never to leave those who believe in Him. Jesus empowers His believers in this world and in His kingdom where He and His disciples will be eternally present, unaffected by time and space. The presence of God in the form of the Holy Spirit is the proof in the believer's life that he/she belongs to God. In obeying the commandments, the believer proves that he/she is God's obedient child and seeks to please God at all times. The Holy Spirit reveals God's divine plans and purposes for the lives of Christians. Each believer is tasked with revealing God who dwells within, not relishing in the gifts that has been bestowed upon him/her but to use them for God's kingdom building. The believer's sterling contribution to building the church is recorded in heaven.

"Thy kingdom come," we often recite in the Lord's Prayer. As Christians, we have the power to bring God's kingdom into existence here on earth. God's kingdom comes whenever we allow our spiritual gifts to point to Christ. When we employ these gifts to help fellow Christians, a neighbor (who is anyone in need), teach our children, feed the hungry, visit the sick and those imprisoned, heal, preach the Word of God, we establish the kingdom of God. These are a few of the ways we can allow God's kingdom to come to earth as it is in heaven. Exercise our spiritual gifts and bring joy and comfort to the world—it is God's will and purpose for every inspirited believer. We do not do this work by ourselves; it is the Holy Spirit living within us that gives us the power to accomplish the great commission. The great commission was directed to the disciples by Jesus as He prepared to ascend to God (Acts 1:8). The mandate is for disciples of Christ to take the good news of His suffering and resurrection to all the world. Winning souls for God is paramount and—in the event that one accepts Jesus as Lord—gives cause for great rejoicing in heaven. This fact is revealed in Jesus' Parable of the Prodigal Son (Luke 15).

Being filled with the Holy Spirit is supernatural, not superstition. The Spirit working in believers equips them to move beyond boundaries developed geographically, socially, economically, ethnically, and perceptively. Jesus taught us that there are no boundary lines when serving Him, whether performing miracles or preaching the good news of the gospel of salvation. There is room for everyone in the household of God. With Christ as the chief cornerstone, we all, with varying gifts, build the body of the church one brick at a time. Every brick is important regardless of size, shape, or similarity.

The Bible is a great example of this concept of unity in diversity. The four gospels were written by four distinct authors who set out to tell the good news of Jesus Christ and His salvation. They were often similar in their records of Jesus' words and actions, especially among the gospels of Matthew, Mark, and Luke, often referred to as the Synoptic Gospels. On the other hand, John depicted Jesus on a more spiritual plateau especially in his introduction, declaring Jesus as the Word made flesh. Each writer brought his individual characteristic in his contribution to the gospel story, and we know that the Holy Spirit inspired them, but He permitted each to present what he thought was significant and important to salvation. Thus, each gospel appeals to various peoples and their cultures. Matthew's gospel can easily appeal to someone of the Jewish faith whose religious roots reach back to Abraham, the father of faith. Luke's record is thorough in including the then Greco-Roman culture of the day, giving a vivid description of the political parity and its intertwining with the fulfillment of the Jewish prophecies. Mark is youthful and "pulls no punches." He tells it as he sees it and describes in simple language the rapid, wonderful deeds of Jesus. Many scholars believe that Mark was the first gospel to be recorded. John's gospel is deeply spiritual, announcing the Word as God and life and is the source of this very book from which I proclaim God's makeover of all who believe in Him (see "Inspiritation"). Christians must never let their varied spiritual gifts be in competition or be evaluated but should employ these spiritual gifts as a means by which God Almighty alone is glorified (*sola gloria*).

A Spirit-filled believer masters the art of listening to God. For in developing a keen spiritual ear, he/she can exercise the will of God and develop the divine nature where one may receive God's instructions and the means by which miracles manifest. The little lad Samuel heard God calling while he slept. The priest Eli realized after the third call that it was God communicating with the lad (1 Samuel 3). Abraham heard God's call to sacrifice his son, Isaac, on Mount Moriah, and although it may have been emotionally very painful, this father of faith obeyed and went about the business early the next morning (Genesis 22:3). This is why the Scripture informs that God desires obedience rather than sacrifice. Spiritual listening is an art that all believers should strive to cultivate and acquire as an attribute. Hence, so it is with the Holy Spirit dwelling within the believer who matures the believer to become conscious of his workings. This consciousness develops obedience to the Holy Spirit's instructions, regardless of how simple or awkward His instructions may be.

Hence, without the Holy Spirit, one is as dead because to live under the flesh produces death, but the Spirit gives life. As in the vision in the book of Ezekiel, the dry bones of the valley did not rise up and live until the breath of God entered those bones (Ezekiel 37:9–10). The breath of God is the Holy Spirit who gives life and hope to the flesh. As Paul reminds us that a life lived under the Holy Spirit is alive and free of condemnation (Romans 8:1). This is the wonderful life as against a life filled with the amenities of the world, which often offers fleeting satisfaction and a life void of depth and purpose. This is why the wealthy young man in the Gospel of Luke went away despondent when Jesus suggested that he sell his goods and distribute the proceeds to the poor (Luke 22). Nothing is wrong with riches rightfully gained and purposefully put to use in the manifestation of the kingdom of God. The indwelling Holy Spirit empowers the mind to behold the plans of God and to be conscious of His abundant blessings which when shared produces peace and joy in this life and eternal dividends in the life to come. Paul invites all to renew our minds by the Spirit who encourages Christians to lose their grip on the blessings they have received but deposit them so that they may multiply exponentially (Ephesians 4:23).

It is imperative that the born-again comprehend that all potentials are conceivable. Even though some may be perplexing, he/she must be content under all. This contentment is part of the possibilities because of faith. For it is written, "But without faith it is impossible to please him: for he that cometh to God must believe that he is, and that he is a rewarder of them that diligently seek him"

(Hebrews 11:6). Therefore, nothing should stand in the way of faith, which is also worship. In addition, faith leads to endurance, and endurance produces spiritual maturity that serves as witness for Christ who promises to be with His children. During times of the difficult situations, the Christian's faith, thus exercised, is on display for all to witness and propels one to greater spiritual heights. Under these circumstances, the Christian relies totally on the Holy Spirit's power to preside over the possibilities, thus igniting God's presence and ability to represent him/her.

Jesus' instructions to Nicodemus—that he must be born again—nurtured Nicodemus into receiving the Holy Spirit. How do we know that Nicodemus received the Holy Spirit? The answer lies in his work—work that can only be ignited by the instructions of the Holy Spirit. This work propelled Nicodemus to provide one hundred pounds of myrrh and aloes to anoint his master's body. Along with Joseph of Arimathea, he prepared the body of Jesus for burial and laid it in a new tomb (John 19:39–41). It is a great difference from his former visit by night to see Jesus to openly take care of the body of Christ—an honored opportunity. The inspirited Nicodemus was now not ashamed to be associated with Jesus. He performed his duty in broad daylight. Such is the work the Holy Spirit allows in our lives, when we as Christians, believe and develop our spiritual eyes, ears, and intellect to His authority. The Spirit-filled life moves Christians beyond their comfort zone and compels them to perform great acts of kindness with all their being. Nicodemus's darkness became light, and he subsequently saw God's light which primed him for the privilege of participating in the drama of Christ's salvific achievement. Nicodemus and Joseph became spiritual priests who attended the temple of God. Jesus referred to His body as this temple when He stated, "Destroy this temple, and in three days I will raise it up" (John 2:19). Subsequently, those who are born again become the temple of God because of the Holy Spirit dwelling within them. This reality of the temple and the Holy Spirit were given in a vision by an angel to Ezekiel, where this divine duo metaphorically portrays water flowing out from the temple's threshold, increasing from a stream to a river and nourishing everything in its path (Ezekiel 47).

To be born again means that the Holy Spirit has occupied our entire being. No department of our lives is without the Spirit's accessibility; partial occupancy is not an option. While the human nature is prone to sin which leads to death, the Holy Spirit from above produces life. "The Holy Spirit has been given in part, to guide us into all truth" (Jeremiah 2014).[7] And again, according to John's gospel, all who believe in God are His children (John 1:12).

The Holy Spirit guides, directs, protects, corrects, reveals God's will for our lives, counsels, strengthens, leads, communicates, and flourishes us. A sister in Christ who has formed a prayer session by telephone every Sunday evening confessed that God had prompted her to formulate this praying community. She hesitated and allowed her other obligations to impede God's request. However, she stated that one night she had a dream that she was pregnant, but

---

[7] David Jeremiah, *Quest: Seeking God Daily*, daily devotions, February 22.

she could not feel any movement of the baby, so she went to a doctor. She awoke from her sleep just then and wondered what this dream meant. It was revealed to her that she had neglected to obey the Holy Spirit in establishing a prayer line that is now in existence and brings comfort and solace to the women who participate.

Jesus' confirms the meaning of new birth by declaring He is not going to leave us as orphans. Orphans are children without parents or parental guidance. Thus, Jesus' statement verifies that those who believe on Him are born into a spiritual family with God as our spiritual parent. Whether our biological parents are alive or dead, Christians have a spiritual parent who is eternal. Hence, we are never orphans under the new birth. Jesus defines the parameter of His family when He declared that those who do the will of His Father is qualified to be family, and the Father's will is revealed through the Holy Spirit (Mark 3:35). The Reverend Charlie Holt describes the defects of the natural family in creating pride and confusion: "When humans go to war, it is often because they find their identities in their natural families or human ancestry... The worst factions of any on earth are factions in and among families" (Holt 2015).[8] When families take pride in the pedigree of human nature, discrimination, division, and dissension sow discord and ill will. In contrast, families born of the Holy Spirit can boast in nothing but love and live to demonstrate that love of God and to the world. This fact of new birth expounded by the apostle Paul encourages people to

---

[8] Charlie Holt, *The Crucified Life: Seven Words from the Cross*, page 84.

put away the old natural nature and embrace the new creation in Christ (2 Corinthians 5:17).

The power of the Holy Spirit was on display when He manifested His ability to fill a yet-unborn baby, John the Baptist, while yet in his mother Elizabeth's womb, causing him to leap for joy at the sound of the Blessed Virgin Mary's salutation to Elizabeth. The baby's response let his mother know assuredly that God chose Mary to be the mother of the long-expected Messiah (Luke 1). Of course, the infiltration of the Holy Spirit is always significant and purposeful as the apostle Paul reiterates, "To each individual the manifestation of the Spirit is given for some benefit" (1 Corinthians 12:7). Therefore, the Christian cultivates and develops communication with the Holy Spirit in order to execute the command of God whether for wisdom, knowledge, faith, healing, prophecy, or the gift of speaking in another language and its interpretation. The purpose of the Holy Spirit is crucial and serves as a guaranty against false claims and haughty practices. The purpose lies in the Word of God because the Word spoken since the beginning created life, and the creation continues anew through the inspiritation of those born-again.

Prayers as well as rest sharpen and enlighten human nature to discern and obey the instructions of God. Utilizing the mind as the source of spiritual vision is a practice of meditation and is what theologians refer to as divine revelation. The eye of the Spirit is the mind. The born-again believer must use the mind to see only possibilities. Those who are born-again Christians use faith to see the possibilities of the vision of God's plan and directives, a vision which consists of the present and the future. Past incidents and the manner they were handled while the Christian was in the flesh may often produce regrets and a sense of shame. The power of the Holy Spirit living within urges us to leave those times behind and dwell within the present while reaching forward to the future. The apostle Paul is a good example of this dilemma as he forgot his past deeds against God and His people and concentrated on his new state as a child of God. "Just one thing: forgetting what lies behind but straining forward to what lies ahead (Philippians 3:13).

Several athletes carry the Olympic torch across the globe, each taking a turn until it reaches the host city. Similarly, inspirited Christians perform the work of God. They witness to the light in many places and varied ways and, like the athletes, pass the torch on at the end of their earthly journey. Jesus' death on the cross two thousand years ago brings life and light to millions through the ages and up until this present time so that the flame of our Lord never dies. Some Christians live a long period while others only for a short time. However, in God's arena, there is no time. So whether long or short, all their works witness to the glory of God. Jesus always kept God, His Father, in focus. As Paul writes, "For we are his handiwork, created in Christ Jesus for the good works that God has prepared in advance, that we should live in them" (Ephesians 2:10).

Some believers are wealthy on earth while others barely exist from day to day. The inspirited accepts the lot that is assigned—be it a life of glory or the quiet mundane repetitive task, unnoticeable but necessary for the daily seamless operation of caring services for humanity. Nevertheless, in the life after death, these conditions change to the eternal enigma where the poor loses poverty and the rich is relieved of worldly wealth. All are then level under a new preternatural paradigm in paradise.

Suffering is part of life, and one day, my faith was sorely tested when my son left with his brother-in-law and never returned. They both died in a tragic car accident. My son-in-law had invited my son to go out with some friends. The night prior to the accident, I requested that he gave me a wake-up call at five o'clock in the morning in order to be on time for Bible study meeting at seven o'clock in the morning. He then gave me a weird look—one I will never forget (as if to say he would not be here) and instead told his father on his way out the door to give me the wake-up call. On their way home, his car slammed into a railroad concrete column and burst into flames. Their bodies were burned beyond recognition and subsequently had to be buried in sealed caskets. They died in the early morning while I was at the prayer meeting. We had just finished studying Romans chapter 8, and in retrospect, I think God was preparing me for the devastating news.

I returned home to find my husband relaxing, oblivious to what had happened. I began receiving a number of calls from relatives who realized I had not yet heard and stopped short of telling me. Finally, my daughter arrived with a cousin and a security guard. They asked me to sit in a chair outside of the house and broke the news. I felt numb, no feelings at all. I did not believe what they were telling me. My husband was never the same after that fatal day and subsequently suffered from health issues.

I have tasted the bitterness of tragedy and suffering, but God in His merciful goodness has granted me the strength to carry on. At the time of the tragedy, I felt the power of the prayers and those of my relatives, friends, and the four hundred women of the Bible study. God has sustained me and given me strength to bolster my husband and daughter. The strength came from God Almighty and has become my testimony of His love and mercies. When I returned to work, my co-workers were all observing me; some spoke words of comfort while others remained quiet. I found strength from serving others and know firsthand about the comfort found in service (Acts 20:35).

The suffering of the born-again believer witnesses to others in various ways. A few months after the loss of my son and son-in-law, a co-worker lost her young daughter from a heart condition. After she returned to work, she relayed that all through her grieving, she thought of me and how my example of faith and perseverance gave her the strength to cope with her grief.

Evidence

The evidence of inspiration is recorded in the Scripture which related how Philip, directed by an angel to travel on a road that led from Jerusalem to Gaza, met the treasurer of the Ethiopian queen. The Spirit instructed Philip to embark this official's chariot and minister to him that Jesus is whom the Prophet Isaiah prophesied about in his book. The official requested to be baptized and obviously became a disciple (Acts 8:36). The conversion of this eunuch, most likely, is the beginning of the Ethiopian orthodoxy and demonstrates the responsibility of each disciple to evangelize.

During my school years, I was often puzzled when fellow students would ask, "Are you born-again?" I wondered how I may answer their question. Today, the answer is a resounding yes. I was born again when I received the Holy Spirit at my baptism and made a child of God and ratified at the sacrament of confirmation as a young adult. To be born again should be the goal of every follower of Christ. This motivation needs not be driven by a desire to exercise authority in the church or community but to serve humanity with zeal and affection. Service to humanity is rooted in the fact that Jesus at the end of His days on earth declared, "I give you a new commandment; love one another. As I have loved you, so you also should love one another. This is how all will know that you are my disciples, if you have love for one another" (John 13:34–35). The love we share for one another as Christians should be the example of the intense love God has lavished over us. Jesus declared, "I will not leave you orphans; I will come to you." He has come to us through the power of the Holy Spirit. Jesus' wonderful love is expressed in many and varied ways that most times we are not even conscious of it.

The faith record of Shadrach, Meshach, and Abednego serves as an exemplary example. These young men were content to accept whatever fate God had planned for them when they boldly refused to worship King Nebuchadnezzar's golden idol even under the threat of his pronouncement of a fiery death. In addition, their faith boldly confessed before the king of their uncertainty of God's plan to have them either survive or succumb to the flames of the furnace. These men were prepared to experience whatever possibility deemed fit by God. God acted, and they survived and caused this pagan king to praise God (Daniel 3). It would do well for the disciple to know that the third day (the day of victory over evil) will always arrive and on God's timing. Be aware that it is God's prerogative to punctuate the possibility at hand, managing it in whichever way He deems fit. The disciple's duty is to pray, watch, and wait, for this is the essence of faith.

Similarly, the pleasant possibilities summons the born-again to not only enjoy but also acknowledge God's graciousness and saving justice. Thus, the disciple pens a song of thanksgiving to God for all generations to sing with exultant joy and greatness. Pleasant possibilities witness as well to God's sovereignty and should be a time of expressing humility. In this jubilant state, thanksgiving to God is important, lest temptation seduces the born-again to become boastful or to claim God's handiwork as one's own. As the book of Psalms invites the disciples, "Come, let us sing joyfully to the Lord" (Psalm 95:1). Praises and psalms to God are essential in telling the story of God's saving justice and leaving a legacy of faith to witness to the unsaved.

Meanwhile, it is incumbent that the disciple tells the story of God's love and grace which testifies to unbelievers. Their testimony and song of praise may prompt unbelievers to become disciples, thus enlarging the kingdom of God "on earth as it is in heaven" (Matthew 6:10). The pleasant prospects demand similar faith as those that are exasperating and difficult. The Magnificat, known as the song of the Virgin Mary, attests to God's power and her faith in the fulfillment of His promise to make her the mother of the Messiah (Luke 1:46–55).

As a newborn baby needs milk, so the novice Christian needs the Word of God in order to thrive. By constantly studying the Word of God—the Bible—the new disciple grows into maturity and becomes gifted and competent in deciphering sound doctrine. This growth attributes to the council of the Holy Spirit who operates as the teacher and counselor. Constant prayer, meditation, and fasting are conducts that cause a Christian to mature in spirituality that cultivates a comprehensive communication with God. A spiritual communication that is never self-serving and self-seeking nor promotes or glorifies the newborn as privileged or special in the eyes of others. Instead, the spiritual intelligence of the disciple seeks to glorify God and humbly strives to expand God's kingdom here on earth by obedience to God's commands—to wash one another's feet.

The disciple of Christ will do well to recall the instruction of the Scripture, "For our struggle is not with flesh and blood but with the principalities, with the powers, with the world rulers of this present darkness, with the evil spirits in the heavens" (Ephesians 6:12). Therefore, it is essential that the disciple uses the weapons of the Spirit—that is, the Word of God, faith, and constant prayers to demolish the stronghold of evil. The Holy Spirit empowers the disciple to win the war by offering up prayers on his/her behalf, thus witnessing to the power of God and the fact that God never lets His children's enemies overpower them. The Spirit's prayer to God on behalf of the disciple uplifts his/her human nature when it agonizes and experiences overwhelming circumstances that may cause torment and distress which can easily lead to depression. Under these circumstances, care must be taken for the human nature of the born-again to relinquish its endeavors and allow the Holy Spirit to have His sway. The language used in prayer by the Holy Spirit on behalf of the believer is indiscernible and inaccessible by human wisdom.

The incarnation of Jesus is substantiated for a second time when, at His baptism, the Trinity (the divine holy family) is present. The Holy Spirit descended in the form of a dove upon Jesus (the Son), and God the Father declared, "You are my beloved Son, with you I am well pleased" (Luke 3:23). Similar procedures occur when a person receives the Holy Spirit; God rejoices that one chooses to be born again. The person whom God created exercised his/her free will to trust in the power of the Holy Spirit. It is a decisive decision to be born again.

God is preparing your new bodies. It was essential for Jesus to retain His crucifixion marks which serves as witness to His great love for the human race and His victory over death. His marked body resides in heaven where our new bodies are being tailored for a perfect fit at the second coming of Jesus. Those who have suffered from molestation, rape, illness, and any form of abuse take heart, for this body will be replaced new and whole resplendent in glory and beauty. Hence, the scars of Jesus' body will make our bodies whole and scar free. Meanwhile, each time you tend to recall the scars on your body caused by a perpetrator, the believer may train the mind to cover those wounds with the wounds of Jesus. Jesus invited doubting Thomas to touch His wounds, and so He invites all who are hurt and in doubt to do the same. The apostle Peter explains, "He himself bore our sins in his body upon the cross, so that, free from sin, we might live for righteousness. By his wounds you have been healed" (1 Peter 2:24). Note that Peter uses the past perfect tense; the healing is already accomplished. Reach up and claim your healing.

Jesus invites Thomas and us to touch his wounds. They are real, and from this tender invitation to touch, our wounds are healed and removed because his wounds remain. Feel free to touch Christ's wounds and find healing for your own. Jesus' wounds are witness to His winning and to all those who believe as well.

God has given us a spirit and a body at creation (Romans 1:20). However, disobedience by Adam and Eve in Eden produced the destruction of the body and dulled the spirit. God is determined to have not only the spirit which is indestructible but the entire composition which He created in the beginning—the body and the spirit to be reinstated. For this very reason, God sent His only begotten Son Jesus Christ to dress in human flesh so that He may transform our human nature in making it fit for God's kingdom dwelling. Jesus then informs Nicodemus that he must be born again so that, after his resurrection, the Holy Spirit will empower human nature and thus accomplish the total makeover.

The kingdom of God is far superior to the riches and things of this world. But there is order here. Believers must seek the things of God's kingdom first, and then the things of this world will follow. The visible elements—such as food, drink, or goods—are subservient to the reality of the unseen (Luke 12:29–32). In placing the unseen first and foremost as desirable, then worldly things become reality.

John chapter 3 fulfills the entire Old Testament. In this chapter, particularly verse 16, the gospel summarizes the good news of God. Additionally, in this chapter, Jesus is presenting Nicodemus and all who chose to believe in Him their citizenship papers. Jesus knew that He came for the purpose of calling humanity back to the status that God had intended for us to enjoy—the status Adam and Eve experienced before the fall. It grieved God that He had to expel His prime creation from the wonderful life He intended for humanity to experience. Sin separated a holy God from His beloved creation. Subsequently, God devised a plan to reestablish this lost relationship by sending prophets, judges, and kings to show humanity His divine love. Many of these messengers proved unsuccessful in convincing humankind and were misunderstood and often killed.

Finally, God sent His only begotten Son Jesus to convey His love and plan to reunite humanity to Himself. His Son was misunderstood as well, and humanity called for His death while releasing a murderer. Jesus was conscious of God's divine plan and endured death on the cross. For this purpose, Jesus destroyed death by His death. Jesus destroyed this enemy forever and obtained life for all who placed their faith in Him.

Through Jesus' resurrection, He gifted humanity with the presence of the Holy Spirit. Through the Holy Spirit, humanity is under a new birth—a revised status. This new status is what Jesus referred to as born-again—the key to a new relationship with God, thus ending the severed one. Humanity is now inspirited, restored to power and kingdom citizenship. Thus, it is the duty of every new citizen to tell others of this wonderful grace that God has given to all and that each human being has the opportunity to retrieve his/her citizenship papers and live in God's kingdom here on earth and in heaven. There is no other option for being a part of God's kingdom—one must be born again. Praise be to God.

References

Aquinas, T. 1964. Summa Theologiae: Cambridge University Press: Cambridge, UK.

Chambers, Oswald. 2000. *My Utmost for His Highest: Selections for the Year*. Ohio: Barbour & Co.

Church of England. 1992. *The Book of Common Prayer*. Ebury Press.

Holt, Charlie. 2015. *The Crucified Life: Seven Words from the Cross*. Florida: Bible Study Media.

Jeremiah, David. 2014. *Quest: Seeking God Daily*. California: Turning Point.

O'Collins, Gerald. 2013. *Christology: A Biblical, Historical, and Systematic Study of Jesus*. Oxford: Oxford University Press.

Senior, Donald, John Collins, and Mary Ann Getty. 2011. *The Catholic Study Bible*. Oxford: Oxford University Press.

The Bible, Authorized King James Version, 1976. Tyndale House Publishers Inc.

About the Author

Bernice Austin-Brutus hails from Georgetown, Guyana, where she worked in the Public Service and the Central Bank of Guyana. Bernice migrated to the United States in 1983 and lived in New York City where she worked as a legal administration assistant with the Port Authority of New York and New Jersey before relocating to Stone Mountain, Georgia. She is recently widowed after being married for forty-four years to the late Albert R. Brutus. Bernice obtained a Masters in Theology from Saint Leo University in Florida. She taught adult Sunday school for several years at Rock of Ages Lutheran Church and was part of the church council serving in the community involvement ministry and volunteers with the clothes closet and food for the homeless ministry. She is presently retired as a financial specialist after twenty-four years of service with the Metropolitan Atlanta Rapid Transit Authority. She resides near her daughter, Jonelle, and two teenage grandchildren.

CPSIA information can be obtained
at www.ICGtesting.com
Printed in the USA
BVHW061143080222
628386BV00013B/985